CHAIR,
NATIONAL BOARD
OF DIRECTORS

Patricia Diaz Dennis

CHIEF
EXECUTIVE
OFFICER

Kathy Cloninger

EXECUTIVE
VICE PRESIDENT,
MISSION TO MARKET

Norma I. Barquet

VICE PRESIDENT,
PROGRAM
DEVELOPMENT

Eileen Doyle

WRITERS: Jennifer Goddard, Karen Unger, Jan Herman, Kelli Martin, Monica Shah, Valerie Takahama
CONTRIBUTOR: Kathleen Ferrier
ILLUSTRATED BY Billie Jean
DESIGNED BY Parham Santana

© 2008 by Girl Scouts of the USA

First published in 2008 by Girl Scouts of the USA
420 Fifth Avenue, New York, NY 10018
www.girlscouts.org

ISBN: 978-0-88441-719-4

Printed in Italy

1 2 3 4 5 6 7 8 9/16 15 14 13 12 11 10 09 08

contents

4   A Is for..

28   Shout It Out for Advocacy

36   Step 1: Find Your Cause

48   Step 2: Tune In

58   Step 3: Harmonize

66   Step 4: Identify the Big Ears

74   Step 5: Plan the Perfect Pitch

86   Step 6: Raise Your Voice,
         Make Your Pitch

90   Step 7: Close the Loop

94   Step 8: Reflect, Reward, Celebrate

A IS FOR...

AMBASSADOR,
A GIRL WHO CHANGES THE WORLD.

As a Girl Scout Ambassador, you know leadership from the inside out:

You believe in yourself, your abilities, and your values.

You know how to team up and build a network.

And you know the world can be better.

So you do what it takes to make a difference.

You become an advocate.

A is for Ambassador, the highest rank in Girl Scouting. B is for Bravo!—for making it this far.

Journey forward!

You've heard about the effects of random acts of kindness: You help someone cross the street. A driver sees your kindness and lets a car into a crowded traffic lane. The driver of that second car then holds the door open for a mother struggling with packages and small children. That mother stops to help a crying child find her father at the playground. That father helps someone cross a street. And on it goes. Small acts ripple out, ultimately creating major whirlwinds of change.

On this journey, you will create your own little whirlwind. How? By being an advocate. That means lifting your voice as a force for positive change in the world.

A is for advocate, someone who speaks up for lasting change.

B is for butterfly, a powerful symbol of transformation.

Here's how the two come together:

Scientists tell us that the world of nature is so small and interdependent that a butterfly flapping its wings in the Amazon rainforest can generate a violent storm on the other side of the Earth. Today, we realize, perhaps more than ever, that the world of human activity also has its own "Butterfly Effect."

— Kofi Annan, accepting the Nobel Peace Prize in 2001

Advocate comes from the Latin word for voice. To be an advocate is to raise your voice on behalf of others to achieve, or at least strive for, lasting change. Advocates get at the root of a problem. They zoom in on one critical angle of it and create a plan to address it. Advocates then pitch that plan to those with the influence to make lasting change.

Around the world, teens like you and people younger and older are raising their voices as advocates. They're speaking out on causes they believe need help: global warming, universal health care, racism, child poverty—whatever they're passionate about. On this journey, you, too, will see that your voice is powerful enough for just about anything you believe in.

Why isn't there a later bus for people who have after-school sports and clubs? Someone should get us a new bus schedule!

It scares me how many car accidents my friends were in this year. Someone needs to do something about DUI drivers around here!

Did you see that movie about global warming? Scary! What policies is our city putting in place to combat global warming?

SAY WHAT? CAN'T HEAR YOU YET!

Speaking up doesn't necessarily mean speaking to a crowd. Sometimes you just need to speak up to a few people—those in a position to really do something! And the issue you speak up about doesn't have to be big. It might be something small, and right in your backyard. Can you think of an example? Maybe an issue that hits close to home?

YOU BELONG TO A LONG LINE OF ADVOCATES

When you speak up and speak out, you are joining a league of women who have raised their voices for change throughout history. Women like **Isabella Baumfree**, a slave in upstate New York who took the name Sojourner Truth and traveled widely, giving speeches on the rights of women; **Nellie Bly**, who went undercover to expose the torturous treatment of patients at New York's Women's Lunatic Asylum; **Grace Murray Hopper**, who led the way for women in computer science; **Billie Jean King**, who lobbied for women's right to equal pay in pro tennis and helped end sex discrimination in high school and college athletics; **Betty Williams and Mairead Corrigan**, whose petitions and peace marches against the violence in Northern Ireland led to a Nobel Peace Prize; and **Aung San Suu Kyi**, the 1991 Nobel Peace Prize winner who raised her voice for democratic freedom as Burmese soldiers aimed their guns at her. To learn more about these women, and meet many more outstanding advocates, just flip through this book and check out the Voices for Good section that runs along the bottom of the pages. Read about their issues. What are yours?

advocate extraordinair

Far ahead of her time, Girl Scouts founder Juliette "Daisy" Gordon Low was the ultimate advocate—for girls. She wanted girls all around the world to be fully engaged in productive affairs and to develop to their full potential—physically, mentally, and spiritually. When she assembled 18 girls from Savannah, Georgia, on March 12, 1912, for the first-ever Girl Scout meeting, she had that vision in mind.

Her efforts on behalf of girls led her to partner with leaders across the country and around the world. Within a few years, her dream of a far-reaching, girl-centered organization was a reality.

Today, Girl Scouts of the USA has a membership of 3.6 million girls and adults, and more than 50 million women are Girl Scout alumnae. Girl Scouts is also a member of the global sisterhood of the World Association of Girl Guides and Girl Scouts (WAGGGS). Read more about Daisy Gordon Low on pages 48 and 62. Learn more about WAGGGS on page 40.

CHOOSING YOUR ROUTE TO ADVOCACY

The routes to advocacy are as varied as the causes you care about. But on this journey, advocacy follows eight sequential steps that you can easily fit into your busy life—now and anytime you want to speak up. Each step builds on the one before, giving you new insights, stronger skills, and greater confidence. So decide how you want to journey forward—on your own or with a team. With a team, you can travel the journey one step at a time, exploring the world of advocacy and enjoying breaks with sister Ambassadors. Or you can climb the eight steps in a burst of energy, reflecting on your path in a big way at the end. Either way, if you complete the eight steps to advocacy, the prestigious Girl Scout Advocate Award is yours.

HOW TO RAISE YOUR VOICE IN 8 STEPS

What follows, in a handy chart format, is a rundown of this journey's eight steps to advocacy. Each step is explored in depth in later chapters of this book. Think of this chart as Advocacy Central. Use it and the accompanying pages to keep track of all the new contacts you meet along this journey and what you decide to do together. As you journey forward, all your notes and plans will be right here together.

ADVOCACY CENTRAL

STEP	THE DETAILS	HOW TO ACHIEVE IT	DETAILS FOR MY CAUSE
Step 1: FIND YOUR CAUSE	Investigate issues you care about. Choose one that touches your heart and soul.	Stick to an issue you really care enough about to speak up for and act on—and to influence others to act on.	My issue is And I hope to
Step 2: TUNE IN	Do some research. Zoom in on a specific angle and possible solutions.	Seek out the root causes. Where can you learn more? Consider as many sources of information as possible—the media, people in your community, the Internet. Are your sources trustworthy? Unbiased?	
Step 3: HARMONIZE	Form alliances with those who care about your issue and can assist you in giving voice to solutions.	Find out who else is working on your issue. What advocacy efforts have been effective—or not so effective? Walk in the shoes of someone your issue impacts—or someone who can offer another perspective, perhaps even someone who has tried to address your cause without success. Gather with your partners and cooperate on the next steps.	
Step 4: IDENTIFY THE BIG EARS AND SET UP A MEETING	Join with your partners to identify VIPs (very influential people) who will listen to you and have the influence to lift your cause.	Arrange to meet these VIPs. If possible, attend a public meeting (or two) where you can observe how your potential VIPs make decisions, handle issues, and promote their agenda. Is your issue on their radar? If not, find out how your VIPs take on "new business." Arrange a meeting. Get in touch via phone, e-mail, or a staff member.	

STEP	THE DETAILS	HOW TO ACHIEVE IT	DETAILS FOR MY CAUSE
Step 5: PREPARE YOUR PITCH	Define your issue in a brief and compelling way, and propose a workable solution.	Say why your issue matters. Have a "hook." Propose a solution—make it reasonable, doable, and appealing to the VIPs. Clearly show the benefits— what's in it for you, me, and the community.	
Step 6: MAKE YOUR PITCH	Make your pitch to the VIPs.	Use your confidence. This is it: Your Voice, Your World!	
Step 7: CLOSE THE LOOP AND GIVE THANKS	Now that you've "done" some great advocacy, acknowledge those you've met along the way and pass your efforts forward.	If VIPs jumped onboard based on your pitch, use your thank yous to detail your expectations of what they'll do next for your cause. If they're not onboard, thank them for their time. Are you inspired to go further or have you done all you can? Either way, pass forward your good work—ideas, research, progress—to those who can move it forward even more (partners, school officials, other Girl Scouts, even your VIPs). Use what you've learned to educate and inspire others. How creative can you be in thanking everyone who has supported your efforts?	
Step 8: REFLECT, CELEBRATE	Make sure you take time to reflect on your advocacy journey—all the bumps, valleys, high points, twists, and turns.	How did this effort make you wiser? How will you celebrate your new wisdom?	

My Partners

NAME	CONTACT INFO	NOTES

My VIPs

NAME	CONTACT INFO	NOTES

PREPARE AN INVITATION TO SEND TO YOUR VIPs

MEETING DATE AND TIME:

MEETING LOCATION (ADDRESS/DIRECTIONS):

MEETING PURPOSE (BRIEF OVERVIEW OF ISSUE):

AGENDA (TOPICS TO BE DISCUSSED):

ADDITIONAL NOTES/DETAILS FOR YOU AND YOUR PARTNERS
(SUGGESTIONS FOR NUTRITIOUS SNACKS/REFRESHMENTS TO BRING):

ADVOCACY TO-DO LIST: KEEPING TRACK OF TASKS AND WHO'S DOING THEM

TASK	WHO DOES IT?	WHEN?

OK, you hate that your school can't seem to find a way to sell snacks that are tasty and not so bad for you. If you followed

find your **cause**

1. You've got your cause: nutritious food for all!

tune in

2. Dig up all you can about prepackaged, healthful snack options. Find out which items other schools in your area offer, and the cost. Check out vending machines at area health clubs and gyms. Find out who services them. Survey students, school staff, and/or parents: What would they want?

har-monize

3. Reach out to potential partners—fellow students, parents, the PTA, your principal, the cafeteria staff, pediatricians, dieticians, local hospitals, snack distributors—basically anyone who might join your cause. Hang posters at school or publicize your efforts through the school paper or Web site. The goal? A core group of partners to team up with.

ID the big ears and set up a meeting

4. Gather your new partners and decide on your issue's critical VIPs. Do you need school-board approval for the changes or do officials at your school oversee the decision? Do you need student-council approval first? Attend some meetings of those VIPs. This might mean starting with your student council and moving up the

---

VOICES FOR GOOD: WOMEN ADVOCATES THROUGH THE YEARS

1792

Mary Wollstonecraft publishes her best-known work, *Vindication of the Rights of Women*, which argues that women deserve the right to an education. Educated women would not be seen as naturally inferior to men, she writes.

THE 8 STEPS MIGHT LOOK LIKE

the "8 Steps to Advocacy," would you be able to taste success? Here's a quick soup-to-nuts approach:

chain of command to a school-board meeting. Learn how each official body does business and makes decisions.

5. Figure out what to say, how to say it, and who's best to say it. One or more students? A pediatrician? Some parents? A panel with some of each? Consider using key statistics and studies to enhance your pitch—maybe even a PowerPoint presentation. How much time will you have? You may need to write to the VIPs to request to appear at one of their scheduled meetings or to ask how you can get some "air time." What questions will VIPs have for you? How will you answer?

6. Practice, practice, practice—and then deliver your pitch with gusto!

7. Pass the baton to partners or VIPs. Thank the VIPs for their time—and do it promptly. Let them know what you think could happen next.

8. Step back and evaluate. How did your pitch go? Maybe your soufflé rose to dramatic heights—or just an inch or two? Either way, congratulations! You took a stand and presented your case. Sit back and enjoy a snack.

Mary Mason Lyon, a Massachusetts schoolteacher, founds Mount Holyoke Female Seminary, the first American four-year college for women. It has fewer than 80 students in its first year, but is flooded with so many applicants the next year that some must be turned away. Now known as Mount Holyoke College, it is the oldest of the nation's "seven sisters" liberal-arts colleges for women.

Notice how each of the eight steps to advocacy builds on the one before. Can you imagine how this journey through these eight steps will change you? In what ways?

....

....

....

....

How will the network of partners you form help you in your life?

....

....

....

....

How will it feel to know some VIPs in your community?

....

....

....

....

How do you imagine using your newfound advocacy expertise long after this journey ends?

....

....

....

....

think

A is for **astute**, because you've got the brains to get at the roots of your issue. **A** is for **A-ha!**—you know what you want to change! **A** is for **align** your goals realistically with your other commitments. **A** is for **ascertain**, which is all about figuring out solutions. **A** is for **accomplishment**. You can get it done. **A** is for **action**, which you need to take to **achieve** your **aim**. **A** is for **appetite**, which changing the world works up. **A** is for **allies**, whom you'll meet along

A IS FOR ADVOCATE, SOMEONE WHO SPEAKS UP FOR LASTING CHANGE.

the way. **A** is for **advice**, something you can ask for when you need it. **A** is for **advertise**—tell your friends and family what you're up to. **A** is for **acknowledge** the surprisingly large number of people you have in your circles to **assist** you. **A** is for **accessories**—go ahead and wear some. **A** is for **applause**, which you'll hear a lot of as you find your voice—and your power. **A** is for **achieve**—and you will! **A** is for **adventure**—get going!

TEENS ON TARGET

Still not convinced that you can be an advocate? Consider this: In Bend, Oregon., 10 teens stomped on their doubts and launched Get Outta My Face, a project that aims to put junk-food advertisers on notice and get teens eating right and breaking a sweat. As their Web site says, "We're Gen X, Gen Y and Gen Z and we're not going to sit back and remain the fattest and most unfit generation ever." In their first year, the Oregon teens started a nonprofit organization and began a campaign to collect, from young people across the country, 10,000 short digital media projects (why not use the same medium advertisers use?) that promote smart food and lifestyle choices. Says Judy Shasek, their adult mentor, "A generation of 'tired of being manipulated,' digitally savvy kids . . . is saying, 'Get outta my face and get outta our way!' " Now that's speaking up! Read more about the project at http://get-outta-my-face.com.

ADVOCACY: IT'S FOR EVERYONE

Advocacy happens throughout the world—wherever and whenever people raise their voice to say, "Things don't have to be the way they are—they can be better."

Consider Rosa, 21, of Guatemala. "Before, I was afraid to speak in front of a group," she says. "Now, I swallow my fear and see that I am strong, that my voice should be heard."

Read her story. here

A is for appetite, which changing the world works up!
B is for bountiful, which good snacks ought to be.

VOICES FOR GOOD: WOMEN ADVOCATES THROUGH THE YEARS

1843   **Isabella Baumfree**, a slave in upstate New York who ran off to freedom in 1826, takes the name Sojourner Truth after a religious experience. Celebrated as an abolitionist, she travels widely, giving speeches on the rights of women, black women especially. Her most famous speech, to the Ohio Women's Convention in 1851, is titled "Ain't I a Woman?"

imagine...

living in a beautiful and remote village in Guatemala, so remote you need to cross a big lake in a small boat just to reach the closest town.

growing up speaking a Mayan dialect that only a small group of people in your country speak.

needing to learn Spanish as a second language just to have your voice heard outside your village.

seeing your sister get married at age 14—and seeing all the girls in town leave school at about the same age for early marriages.

imagine...

knowing that this is what your family expects of you.

then, imagine that you...

hear on the radio one day of a meeting about the future of women and girls in your country.

travel alone—to a whole new place—just to attend this meeting.

find an opening in your world—access to new information and ideas!

are excited and nervous, and don't even have enough words to express your feelings.

meet a journalist who speaks your second language, Spanish, and talk with this journalist (and learn what a journalist does) about what is going on in your village and your frustration at why girls don't have more choices, opportunities, and education.

imagine...

this journalist taking an interest in your story and featuring you in her documentary.

traveling to New York for the documentary's premiere. (You've never even been to a big city in your own country.)

meeting people who applaud how you raised your voice—and they are speaking in English, a third language to your ears.

going home and working to start a program to build the self-esteem of girls in your village.

asking the mayor for a safe space to meet.

going door-to-door, telling girls they can dream of a new kind of future—one with education and goals and plans.

Imagine you are Rosa, age 21, a Mayan from Santiago Atitlan, the little village on the far side of the lake.

This is her story.
She is an advocate. She's changing the world.

AMBASSADORS AND ADVOCATES

An ambassador is usually stationed in a foreign capital, but ambassadors are not all stationed abroad. Some have "subject matter" assignments, such as the Ambassador to the United Nations for Economic and Social Affairs. But no matter what her role, an ambassador is an advocate for her country's national interests. At times, leading advocates have been appointed to ambassadorships (one example is Nancy G. Brinker, founder of the Susan G. Komen Race for the Cure—the world's largest breast cancer organization—who served as U.S. Ambassador to Hungary from 2001 to 2003). In short, the skills of ambassadors coincide with those of advocates.

Make it yours.

By the way, two other definitions of ambassador are "an authorized representative or messenger" and "an unofficial representative." How do you, as a Girl Scout Ambassador, act as an ambassador for Girl Scouting—officially and unofficially?

....

....

....

....

VOICES FOR GOOD: WOMEN ADVOCATES THROUGH THE YEARS

1844

Sarah Bagley becomes the first president of the Lowell Female Labor Reform Association, organized by women workers in the textile mills of Lowell, Massachusetts. It is the first American labor group to attempt collective bargaining for better wages and working conditions. The owners refuse to bargain, despite Bagley's testimony before the Massachusetts legislature.

some
Firsts
for u.s. ambassadors

1949 First woman ambassador: Helen Eugenie Moore Anderson, appointed Ambassador to Denmark by President Harry Truman.

1953 First woman career diplomat, Frances Willis, named Ambassador to Switzerland.

1965 First black woman ambassador: Patricia Harris, Luxembourg.

1977 First Hispanic-American woman ambassador: Mari-Luci Jarimillo, Honduras.

1994 First Asian-American woman ambassador: March Fong Eu, Micronesia.

1849 **Harriet Tubman**, a slave in Maryland, flees to freedom in the North. She returns 19 times over the next decade to lead more than 300 slaves to freedom along the Underground Railroad, a secret abolitionist network of "safe houses," earning her a reputation as "the Moses of her people."

As a Girl Scout Ambassador, you've got a lot going on. You're a role model for younger girls and a leader among your peers. Girl Scouts is counting on you to carry its leadership philosophy into the world. That's a tall order! And then there's the whole rest of your life. So at the end of every section of this journey, look for the Take 5 icon. It's an invitation for you and your friends to take time out, kick back, and reflect.

How's your appetite for advocacy and ambassador-ing? How about a few nutritious and yummy snack ideas to keep you energized along the journey?

Apple Snacks: Slice an apple into thin pieces, cover each piece with a thin layer of peanut or almond butter*, sprinkle with cinnamon, and top with dark chocolate or toffee bits.

Gourmet S'mores: Use thin waffle cookies, a bar of artisanal dark chocolate, and a bag of organic marshmallows. Top the waffle cookies with two squares of chocolate and two marshmallows. Zap in the microwave for 10 seconds until the marshmallows puff. Top with another cookie. Eat while warm.

Pumpkin Pie Smoothie: In a blender, combine ½ cup of all-natural pumpkin, 1 tablespoon of cinnamon, ¼ cup of rolled oats, 1 scoop of egg or whey protein (or 1 tablespoon of peanut butter*), 1 cup of water or skim milk, and 3 ice cubes.

* If you're allergic to nuts, substitute yogurt for the peanut butter (so you still get your protein fix!).

How about an Ambassador affair! Everyone brings a dish (or just a snack) a you all settle in for a good talk about all those things you always want t talk about but never find time for.

Make it yours.

Any personal goals waiting on your plate? Things to help jump-start the rest of your life—school projects or college interviews and applications? Can you accomplish any of them on this advocacy adventure? How about improving your community *and* becoming a better public speaker? Or sharpening your persuasive writing skills? Hit the gym more often? Stop procrastinating?

Chat about possible goals with your friends. Get their advice.

Use the space below to jot down anything you want to accomplish on this journey. Visit this page every so often to add in or check off!

I want to _____

_____

_____ **says to try** _____
(friend's name)

_____

MAKING TEAM MEETINGS MEANINGFUL

If you're teaming up with a group of Ambassadors and a Girl Scout adviser, use the planner on the next pages to create ambitious Ambassador gatherings that the entire team will cherish. Every group is unique, so pursue only those ideas that resonate with you and your sister Ambassadors. And no matter what you do, be sure to keep the fun factor high!

Planning Ambassador Meetings

MEETING PLACE: MEETING TIME: ADULT ADVISER(S):

1. TEAMING WITH MEANING

How can we start off our meeting to mark this time together as special?

Who will take the lead and what materials do we need?

2. ADVOCACY IN ACTION

What steps can we take toward completing our advocacy project and earning the Advocate Award?

What information and materials are needed? Who can bring them?

Whom can we invite to help us complete these steps? Who will invite them?

How much time will we spend doing this?

Are there any steps we agree to do on our own before the next gathering? Which?

3. SNACKS AND STRETCHES

Power Snacks: We need them! Who will bring them?

Do any of us want to lead a little stretch break (aerobics, dance moves, yoga, or . . .)?

4. MAKING IT OUR OWN

What ideas from our books or other sources will we want to spend time on?

Do we want to talk about any of the women featured in the book? Does anyone want to research more information about one of the women or another woman?

Which "Make It Yours" sections would be good for a group discussion?

How about careers? Is there someone we want to invite to discuss advocacy careers with us?

5. TAKE 5

Just for fun, it would be great if we could:

6. BEFORE OUR NEXT MEETING

We will have a team planning session to brainstorm our next steps and future meeting plans.

7. THE AMBASSADOR FACTOR

Are we acting like ambassadors among ourselves? How's our teamwork?

Any conflicts or hurt feelings to address? Any affirmations to share about what we admire in each other?

shout it out for advocacy

You use your voice a lot—and not just to shout, sigh, or sing. It's what makes your opinions, beliefs, and passions known. So, how do you use your voice to influence others—for good or bad? Think about times you . . .

- Cheered someone on
- Spread a rumor
- Criticized or made fun of someone (picked on a younger sibling, even?)
- Defended someone
- Spoke up with a great idea
- Got a group to agree

smart

"Never doubt that a small group of thoughtful, concerned citizens can change the world. Indeed, it is the only thing that ever has."

— Margaret Mead, anthropologist, intellectual, and activist; named "Mother of the World" in 1969 by Time magazine

VOICES FOR GOOD: WOMEN ADVOCATES THROUGH THE YEARS

1868 — **Jane Cunningham Croly**, a magazine editor, founds the first professional women's club, Sorosis, after she and other women journalists are refused entry to a program honoring Charles Dickens at the all-male New York Press Club. Croly convenes a national conference of sisterhood groups in 1890, launching an association that still thrives as the General Federation of Women's Clubs.

Now consider these questions:

1. What message does your voice convey to others?

   ....

2. Whom are you influencing, and how?

   ....

3. Are you using your voice to its full potential?

   ....

4. How else could you use your voice?

   ....

SERVICE, ACTION, AND ADVOCACY

You've probably already accomplished a great deal of community service: painting walls or fences, volunteering at an animal shelter, helping an older neighbor. If you volunteered in a soup kitchen, you likely provided a meal and a human touch. Or perhaps you sent money or clothing or other resources to victims of a natural disaster, such as Hurricane Katrina.

Service is often the immediate, and much needed, response to a basic need: food, clothing, shelter, care. You are of service when you feed the hungry, offer clothing to the homeless, or simply help a friend with a tough homework assignment. Being of service is a vital way to help and care.

Still, after your good service ends, the people you help remain in need—possibly on a daily basis. What could you do to address those needs in an ongoing way? How could you get to the root of the issue?

1872 **Susan Brownell Anthony**, cofounder of the National Woman Suffrage Association with Lucretia Coffin Mott and Elizabeth Cady Stanton, tests the ban on a woman's right to vote. She registers and votes in the presidential election (casting her ballot for Ulysses S. Grant, who was running for reelecton). Arrested and brought to trial, Anthony is found guilty. She is fined $100, but never pays the fine.

MOVING TOWARD ACTION

When you move beyond immediate service to understand the root causes of a problem, you move toward action. When you team up and mobilize others in your efforts to find ways to solve that problem, you're connecting and taking action. Your actions can take many forms: petitioning for new traffic-safety laws, creating a center where children who need tutoring can always get it, creating nutritious school-snack options.

Service makes the world better for some people "right now." Action makes the world better for more people for the long term. Sometimes, service and action just naturally blend into one sustainable effort. As a Girl Scout, you use both service and action to live by the Girl Scout Law and "make the world a better place."

ON THE ROAD TO ADVOCACY

Advocacy is a particular kind of action. The goal is to influence policy, whether public or corporate. To do that, you first convince others to join with you on your issue. Then, with your allies, you reach out to those who can do something about the root cause of your issue—the "movers and shakers" who have the influence to make change happen.

Advocacy can be a special, concentrated effort. Or it can be a part of your daily life. Check out the careers list on page 98 to see how many ways you can use advocacy skills in the working world.

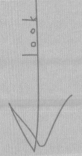

Advocacy Web Sites

Still not exactly sure what an advocate is? Check out these Web sites:

- Youth Venture :
  www.genv.net

- Mobilize.org:
  www.mobilize.org

- Do Something:
  www.dosomething.org

- New Global Citizens :
  www.newglobalcitizens.org

- Idealist:
  www.idealist.org

VOICES FOR GOOD: WOMEN ADVOCATES THROUGH THE YEARS

1881   **Clara Barton**, a teacher and nurse with a long record of humanitarian work during the American Civil War and the Franco-Prussian war, establishes the American Red Cross and becomes its president. Spurred by her idea to offer help not only in wartime but also in any major peacetime disasters, the Red Cross develops into one of the nation's most enduring aid organizations. During her tenure, it aids victims of floods, famine, and earthquakes.

ADVOCACY, PUBLIC POLICY, AND YOU

Being an advocate who influences public policy may not sound exciting—but public policy is powerful. It lays out how individuals and organizations must act. For example, all states have laws or public policies requiring students to attend school (where would you be without those policies?!).

Public policy affects nearly every aspect of life. Every day, you feel the impact of decisions elected officials make at the city, state, and national levels:

- **At home:** The clean water used for your morning shower, the safety of the food you eat, and the energy that powers your home are all regulated by public policy.

- **On the road:** The condition of the streets in your neighborhood, the requirements of your driver's license, the use of bike and motorcycle helmets, and the insurance essentials for your car are all overseen by official bodies.

- **At school:** Mandatory attendance, curriculum requirements, education prerequisites for teachers, the size and location of your school, and the funding for sports and other extracurricular activities—all are set by public policy.

Public policies are set by official bodies, such as school boards, city councils, county boards of commissioners, state legislatures, and Congress. When you advocate, you insert your voice and your unique perspective into the process.

Chloe Dauwalder, Driver-Safety Advocate

Before she was old enough to vote, Chloe was proposing laws in her home state of Utah. At 16, she argued before the Utah State Transportation Committee that a law was needed to require drivers to turn on their vehicle's headlights whenever their windshield wipers were being used.

Chloe had found that 13 states and Canada already had some sort of "Wipe, Shine, and Go" law. So it made sense for a stormy state like Utah to do the same. Chloe's efforts to propose the law earned her the Girl Scout Gold Award—and taught her a lot about the legislative process. "It all was really quite thrilling," she says.

love
this

1884 **Ida Bell Wells** leads a fight against segregation after refusing to give up her seat to a white man when ordered to by a conductor on the Chesapeake, Ohio & South Western Railroad. She is dragged to the "Jim Crow" car at the back of the train by the conductor and two other men. Wells sues the railroad and wins her case, but the decision is reversed by the Tennessee Supreme Court.

You may not instantly get the results you hope for—but by contributing your voice, you participate in shaping policy. Think about it: The more people who participate, the more likely it is that new and innovative solutions will make their way into the world.

When you think about where you might try to use your influence, consider corporate policies as well as public policies. For example, what are supermarkets or other businesses doing to make your community more green? Which policies could the management of those businesses put in place?

Think of a time you provided service. How could you have lifted that service to advocacy?

....

....

....

....

....

....

Make it yours.

think

VOICES FOR GOOD: WOMEN ADVOCATES THROUGH THE YEARS

1887 **Elizabeth Cochrane Seaman**, better known as Nellie Bly, goes undercover, feigning insanity, to investigate the Women's Lunatic Asylum. Her reports in the New York World about beatings, frigid baths, inedible food, and worse cause a sensation. Spurred by Bly's reports, a grand jury conducts its own investigation, resulting in an increase in the city budget for care of the mentally ill.

32

How Influential Are You?

Check the box that best describes your level of community involvement.

		OFTEN	SOMETIMES	NEVER
1.	Vote in a school election			
2.	Run for office or volunteer to serve on a committee (at school or in a community organization)			
3.	Do volunteer/service work in your community (such as rake leaves, shovel snow, tutor others, spend time with seniors)			
4.	Give a speech, make a phone call, or write a letter to someone in your school, community, or state to support or oppose an issue			
5.	Keep up with the news (papers, TV, or online) and discuss it with others			
6.	Start a petition in your school or community organization			
7.	Encourage your parents or other adults to vote in an election; be prepared to vote when you turn 18			
8.	Educate and raise awareness in big and small ways (save paper, recycle, turn off lights)			

A is for alumnae, as in Girl Scout alumnae. B is for benefits—the many that come from being part of this worldwide sisterhood.

Quiz adapted from Take Action! Girls' Pipeline to Power, a grassroots initiative developed by Patriots' Trail Girl Scout Council, Inc. of Boston.

SCORING Give yourself 3 points for every "Often," 2 points for every "Sometimes," and 0 points for every "Never" box you checked.

Look on the bright side: You've been on the sidelines, but by the time you complete this journey, you'll be well on your way to being an advocate.

You are a concerned person and have already taken your first steps toward advocacy. Seize the opportunity offered by this journey to develop your potential.

Wow! You're ahead of the curve and already leading the way! This journey is your dream come true.

How many former Girl Scouts have positions of power and influence in your community? How could you use your Girl Scout connection to bring them around to your cause?

take 5

REFINE YOUR VOICE

With your closest chums, get out a camera phone or video camera and record yourselves speaking up for your cause. Play it back. Do you hear an eloquent, confident voice, or a lot of "ummms," "you knows," and mumbles? Check out the tips on public speaking at www.speaking-tips.com, get advice from your school's drama teacher, and watch some news shows or other public forums. Analyze what makes one person more persuasive than another.

VOICES FOR GOOD: WOMEN ADVOCATES THROUGH THE YEARS

1889

Bertha Felicie Sophie von Suttner publishes *Lay Down Your Arms* "to be of service to the Peace League" and "propagate its ideas." The novel, about the horrors of war, has a huge impact on the public, and she becomes a leader in many pacifist causes over the next 25 years. Von Suttner is awarded the Nobel Peace Prize in 1905. She is the first woman to win it.

Step 1: Find Your Cause

What do you care about? What makes you angry? Worried? Upset? What do you want to change? What do you find wrong and unfair? What do you think could be better?

So many issues, so little time. How's an Ambassador to choose? Turn to page 38 for tips on finding what really fires you up! If a big issue comes to mind, stick with it. As an advocate, you'll zoom in on just one angle of that issue—you won't ever feel overwhelmed.

1889

Ida Bell Wells becomes editor and co-owner of Memphis Free Speech, an antisegregationist newspaper. Her editorials cause her to be driven out of the city in 1892. That year, after the killing of three black businessmen, she publishes the pamphlet, "Southern Horrors: Lynch Law in All Its Phases," and in 1893, along with other black leaders, including Frederick Douglass, organizes a boycott of the Chicago World's Fair over the issue of racism.

COMMUNITY CONNECTIONS

One way to find your cause is to do a little analysis of all of the communities you belong to. Remember: Communities are circles of connection—geographic, cultural, religious, or familial. They can be based on the music you like or the car you drive. Communities can be as small as your circle of closest friends and as large as the millions of Girl Scouts around the world. (Don't forget: You've got sisters in the World Association of Girl Guides and Girl Scouts, too—see page 40.)

VOICES FOR GOOD: WOMEN ADVOCATES THROUGH THE YEARS

Jane Addams cofounds Chicago's Hull House, which revolutionizes neighborhood social services by offering daycare to working moms, night school for adults, an employment bureau, public kitchen, girls' club, library, sports facilities, and health-care help for the poor. After a lifetime of advocacy, Addams is awarded the Nobel Peace Prize in 1931. She is the first American woman to win it.

List or draw all the communities you belong to.
Then think about what matters to the people in
your communities. What do you care enough about
to take a stand on?

Keep in mind that advocacy isn't limited to
communities you already belong to. Advocacy
could make you a member of a new community.
What communities would you like to become a
part of? List or draw them.

As a Girl Scout, you're part of a global community—the World Association of Girl Guides and Girl Scouts (WAGGGS). This umbrella organization for our worldwide sisterhood, with 10 million members, advocates globally on issues of importance to girls and young women. For WAGGGS, advocacy means "speaking, doing, and educating." WAGGGS has six teams at United Nations locations around the world. The WAGGGS UN team at the United Nations in New York works closely with Girl Scouts of the USA. WAGGGS also provides opportunities for international friendship and understanding through travel. Headquartered at the World Bureau in London, WAGGGS owns and operates four World Centers—in England, Switzerland, India, and Mexico. All are open to visits by Girl Guides and Girl Scouts. Read more about WAGGGS at www.wagggs.org.

COMMUNITIES HAVE ISSUES

Now reflect back on your community lists, and consider:

What worries people in your communities? What do they get stressed out about? Are schoolkids sick of all the cigarette butts outside the front doors of their schools? Do they need late buses so they can get home after clubs or sports? What needs have people expressed for the neighborhood: more streetlights, a new stop sign, safer parks?

You get the idea; now figure out what matters to the people in your communities that also matters to you. Go back to your community lists and, next to each, jot down or doodle some ideas about possible issues that may need your voice. (Yes, you can do it!)

And check in with your Girl Scout council. What advocacy issues might your council be involved in right now? Can you join in?

Interesting

VOICES FOR GOOD: WOMEN ADVOCATES THROUGH THE YEARS

1899

Florence Kelley launches the National Consumers' League, which works to persuade the public to buy goods only from companies that meet minimum standards for wages and working conditions. She's also a moving force behind the Pure Food and Drug Act of 1906, which enables federal inspection of meat products and prohibits the making of adulterated food products or poisonous patent medicines.

COMMUNITY MAPPING

Try creating a visual representation of assets and issues in one of the communities you belong to or want to belong to.

- Get out and move. Grab some partners and walk around a neighborhood, school, mall, or other area where you are connected to potential issues. Talk to people.

- Diagram or sketch what you see, feel, and hear as you "walk the beat." Even if you're covering familiar ground, try seeing it through fresh eyes.

- Look for assets and positives—people, organizations, resources—that could be part of the solution to the issue you want to raise your voice for.

IT'S YOUR WORLD—GET TO KNOW IT!

Take some time to read and watch national and international news reports. Surf the Internet for Web sites that reflect international points of view. Expand your awareness of issues that impact the world—and learn of people working on those issues. Explore organizations such as Amnesty International, the Children's Defense Fund, Doctors Without Borders, the Population Council, and Oxfam International to see where and how they are promoting change. Add these worldview issues to your sketches. How do they connect to your local issues?

1902

Ida Tarbell writes a muckraking series of articles in McClure's magazine about the business practices of the wealthiest man in America, the oil magnate and industrialist John D. Rockefeller. In 1904, Tarbell's exposé is published as a book, *The History of the Standard Oil Company*; it leads to the breakup in 1911 of Rockefeller's Standard Oil Trust.

WHAT PULLS YOUR HEARTSTRINGS?

You're now ready to generate a list of **causes you're passionate about.**
Write down all the ideas that have popped into your head—don't stop at the first one!

topic	example
Environment	Propose new environmental protection laws for waterways in your state.
Animals	Petition for "no-kill" shelters in your area.
Youth	Ask the town to budget for more evening hours and a teen lounge at the public library.
Community Health	Work with the parks and other departments to add more bike trails and bike lanes.

VOICES FOR GOOD: WOMEN ADVOCATES THROUGH THE YEARS

1907 **Elizabeth Gurley Flynn**, a union organizer for the Industrial Workers of the World, leads campaigns to organize Pennsylvania garment workers, New Jersey silk weavers, New York restaurant workers, Minnesota miners, and Massachusetts textile workers. In 1920, she helps establish the American Civil Liberties Union, which declares it will defend civil rights guaranteed in state and federal constitutions.

reflection

Now that you've got a list of issues, review your ideas and ask questions, such as:

- Which idea might have an impact on the most people?

- Which idea might require the most resources (which will require the least)?

- Which idea is most realistic, based on my time, energy, and resources right now?

- Which idea would the most people support?

- Which idea has the best chance of success?

- Which idea requires a public-policy solution? What could it be?

- Which idea has other people or organizations already onboard and projects under way? How could I tap into them?

"I've got the issue!"

Fill it in!

PASSION METER

Not every choice or decision can be totally objective. Sometimes, you have to follow your heart. Which idea scores highest on your passion meter? (To be an advocate, you've got to be passionate.)

AND THE WINNER IS . . .

I am an advocate for_____, because_____.

THE INNER ADVOCATE

What's inside an advocate? Qualities and skills and values.

As for qualities, Chloe Dauwalder, the Girl Scout who proposed legislation in Utah (see page 31) says, "Perseverance is a big one for an advocate to have.

"I had to be prepared for people to not want to work with me," Chloe explains, "and for people not to treat me with the respect that someone who is older and more experienced would get. And when people are not receptive to what you need, you just have to keep trying and not really take 'no' as an answer."

VOICES FOR GOOD: WOMEN ADVOCATES THROUGH THE YEARS

1911

Ethel Mary Smyth, a British composer and the first and only woman to have her work performed at the Metropolitan Opera, writes the music for "The March of the Women." Premiered by a chorus of suffragists at London's Albert Hall, it becomes the fight song of the suffrage movement.

Make it yours.

What qualities and skills will you bring to the journey? Persistence? Attention to detail? Speech writing? Public speaking? Do you know anyone who can coach you to develop these qualities? Reach out and ask them for some guidance!

....

....

....

An advocate's issue often ties to her values. What values do you have that influence how you think about what matters in the world?

....

....

Consider the values expressed in the Girl Scout Law. Which value resonates most with you? How do you show it?

....

....

Does this value have something to do with the issue you chose for this journey?

....

....

Which of the Law's values apply to your advocacy effort?

....

....

....

....

The Girl Scout Law

I will do my best to be

honest and fair,
friendly and helpful,
considerate
and caring,
courageous and
strong, and
responsible for
what I say and do,

and to

respect myself
and others,
respect authority,
use resources wisely,
make the world a
better place,
and be a sister to
every Girl Scout.

be a flea?

"If you don't like the way the world is, you change it. You have an obligation to change it. You just do it one step at a time."

—*Marian Wright Edelman*

Edelman grew up in the segregated South, where blacks didn't have equal access to voting, education, or other basic rights. She attended Spelman College, where, in 1959, she became involved in the civil rights movement and was inspired to study law. After graduating from Yale, she became the first black woman to practice law in Mississippi. Her passion for righting wrongs took her to Washington, D.C., where she became counsel to the Poor People's Campaign organized by Dr. Martin Luther King Jr. During this work, her life mission began to crystallize as she realized how vital it was to protect the most defenseless people in society: children.

In 1973, Edelman founded the Children's Defense Fund, which has since become one of the strongest voices advocating for children and families in the nation. The agency documents the problems of, and possible solutions to, children in need. Edelman remains a passionate advocate for children, declaring, "You just need to be a flea against injustice. Enough committed fleas biting strategically can make even the biggest dog uncomfortable and transform even the biggest nation."

[SO AMAZING]

take 5

DISCOVER THE MANY MOODS OF YOU

Ever feel stuck in a rut? Perhaps you often play a certain "role" with friends, at school, or at home: the clown, the worrier, the listener, the decision-maker, the chatty one, the problem-solver, the quiet one?

Next time you're with your friends, family, or your Girl Scout group, try on a new mood. You might find that a new aspect of your inner self makes an appearance.

1. Brainstorm moods (or ways you want to act or social skills you want to try—for a day, week, or month). Write them down.

2. Check out these examples to get you going:

   • Today, I will be calm, like a lake early on a beautiful summer morning.

   • Today, I will speak powerfully, like an ocean.

   • This week, I will be bright, like a full and golden moon lighting the sky.

   • This week, I will have the focus of a microscope.

   • Today, I will be curious, like a child who just traveled somewhere new.

   • Today, I will listen like a stethoscope.

   Notice how these examples are written as affirmations to inspire your confidence:

   > I will _____
   > (No ifs, ands, or buts—you will pull it off!)

3. You've heard of mood rings, right? You put them on and they change color to register your mood. What if YOU decided your mood? Make a mood ring (or bracelet or key chain or patch) and wear it (or attach it to your backpack or wherever). Nothing fancy. Even a scrap of paper that you just carry in your pocket will do!

4. Each week/day/month, wear a different mood and invite friends and family to do the same.

5. Reflect: How do you feel? What did you learn about yourself? How did others react to you and your mood? Was it hard to wear a new mood? Why? Did you like being in this mood? Why?

Step 2: Tune In

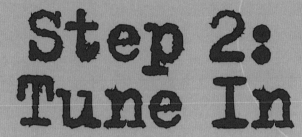

Now that you've selected your issue, it's time to do some research. As you zoom in on particular angles of your issue, what solutions do you see for them? What has already been tried? What would work? Research is important; without it, you'll just be clipping your wings. People might join in with you and care about your issue, but you won't have anything concrete for them to act on. So, here are ways to get the information you need to focus on a specific aspect of your issue—and a possible solution:

BE A DESK JOCKEY

- Use the Internet, magazines, and newspapers to research your issue, solution possibilities, and key players (all potential VIPs).

- Then, get on the phone to talk with parents, teachers, committee members, business leaders, and peers. Keep a notebook of your findings.

INTERVIEW SOMEONE "IN THE KNOW"

- Interview (in person, by letter, e-mail, or phone) an expert on your issue. Prepare questions based on what you

VOICES FOR GOOD: WOMEN ADVOCATES THROUGH THE YEARS

1912 **Juliette Gordon Low** founds Girl Guides (later Girl Scouts) in the United States to promote the social welfare of young women by building self-esteem and teaching such values as courage, honesty, compassion, and good citizenship. Low's project grows into a nationwide movement. By 1919, almost every state has a troop. To date, more than 50 million women have been in Girl Scouts. You're one of them!

think you need to learn about your issue and proposed solutions. This person may also become one of your VIPs.

- Talk to someone on the "other side" of your issue. What's her perspective? How does it impact your possible solutions?

- Try a day (or a few hours) in the shoes of someone directly affected by your issue. Any new perspectives or "aha" moments gained?

RESEARCH POTENTIAL POLICY MAKERS

- Determine whether your issue is a matter of federal, state, or local jurisdiction, or a combination. If you don't know where to start, call the local office of your U.S. senator or representative and ask a staff member for some guidance as to who "owns" the issue.

- Identify a state or municipal policy maker who you feel could help address your issue and put your solutions into action: state senator or other member of the state legislature or assembly, mayor, or city council member.

- Learn about this official's committee assignments, major concerns, background, and voting record (many public officials and policy makers have their own Web sites). Also, many advocacy organizations track how elected officials vote and can provide information about the particular official you're interested in. Create a profile to understand what level of influence the public official might have on your issue and to help you anticipate their views about your concerns.

Capitol Hill here?

A is for astute and B is for the best, both of which your solution just might be.

1914

Jeanette Rankin leads a successful campaign to give women the vote in Montana, six years before the ratification of the 19th Amendment, which grants them that right nationwide. Rankin is elected to the U.S. House of Representatives in 1916, becoming the first female member of Congress. She is still the only woman ever elected to the House or Senate from Montana.

START NETWORKING

- Attend a meeting of an organization or community group that has an interest in, or knowledge of, your issue. Ask for their feedback and take notes—maybe even join! Are there partners or potential VIPs involved in this group whom you might want to tap later?

CONDUCT A SURVEY

- Survey people affected by the issue. Ask them questions based on your proposed solutions. For example, if your issue is creating an accessible playground in a local park, you could ask people who live nearby to respond to statements such as, "An accessible playground should be built in the park" or "The park isn't used enough."

- Record responses on a continuum: strongly agree, agree, disagree, strongly disagree, and undecided. Ask people who they think has the power to make the needed change; they are possible VIPs! (Safety note: Never conduct a survey alone.)

- Analyze your results and present your findings to an organization or group that has an interest in, or knowledge of, the problem. Ask for feedback.

VOICES FOR GOOD: WOMEN ADVOCATES THROUGH THE YEARS

1920   **Carrie Chapman Catt** founds the League of Women Voters as a "mighty political experiment," with the aim of helping newly enfranchised women exercise their responsibilities as voters. No longer limited to female membership—men were allowed to join, beginning in 1973—it is a nonpartisan grassroots organization 150,000-strong, and is perhaps best known for sponsoring the presidential debates of 1976, 1980, and 1984.

50

toward the award

How much research do you need to do? Enough to expand your mind and get the info you need in order to focus on a specific aspect of your issue—and possible solutions.

building a list of allies

Everyone you meet during your research is a potential ally. Some may even be your VIPs. So, while you're researching, you can multitask. Keep a record (in Advocacy Central) of all potential whos—allies and VIPs: their names, snail-mail and e-mail addresses, phone numbers, and notes on their jobs, organizations, and viewpoints. This will come in handy for Steps 3 and 4. And while doing your research, be sure to make a great first impression on anyone you meet!

1923 **Alice Paul**, a founder of the National Woman's Party, drafts the Equal Rights Amendment to end gender discrimination. The amendment has never been enacted. But its main goal—ensuring that all Americans regardless of sex are equal under the law—has been met through judicial decisions involving the Civil Rights Act of 1964 and the Equal Protection Clause of the 14th Amendment, enacted in 1868.

ASSESSING YOUR RESEARCH

Think about what you have learned from your information gathering. At each step, as you gain more information, ask questions that refine your issue and your solution.

- Did I learn something about the issue that I hadn't considered before? What? And why does it matter?

- Is there one angle of the issue that I can focus in on?

- How does the information I gathered offer a possible solution?

- Which sources did I find that are trustworthy and reliable? How can I use their knowledge and legwork to help my efforts?

- What about the people my issue affects? Do they want the solution I am proposing? Are they my allies? If not, how can I make them allies?

- Is this idea the most realistic use of my time and resources?

- Is this solution sustainable? By whom?

- Even if I don't get my solution "passed," will I have made some kind of impact? How?

- Can I be content that I tried my best, even if I don't get the results I wanted?

- Who are the allies I listed? Are any of these people connected in some way?

Make it yours.

If you're like most busy 11th- and 12th-graders, you probably fall asleep late at
night wishing there were more hours in the day. So be realistic about the amount
of time you can spend advocating. In the space below, jot some notes about all the
demands on your time each week: homework, sports, job, chores. Add time crunches
you know will be coming soon: college applications, SATs, prom. Then think about
the time you would like to spend with friends, what your family expects, and any
other demands on your time. (Reality check: There are about 480 waking hours in
a month—720 total hours, less the 240 you'll need for sleeping if you get the
recommended eight hours of zzzs every night.) So, how much time is left for your
advocacy project? What could you do to make more time? Divvy up the project among
friends? Narrow its scope? Spread it out over a longer period?

test
prep

sleep

chores

prom

study

sports

job

homework

With a clear, well-researched idea of the challenges your issue presents and possible solutions that address the root of it, you are so ready for the next step! But first, visit Advocacy Central.

Use the information you've gathered so far to decide what you'll do, and list the steps necessary to reach your goal. For example, if you're concerned about your supermarket using plastic bags (and lots of them), your Advocacy Central chart might include this kind of information:

Step 1:
Find Your
Cause

I worry about all the waste in using plastic bags and how their use in my community contributes to global warming. One example is the supermarket—do we really need to be using all those plastic bags?

Step 2:
Tune In

The supermarket could have giveaway days when customers receive reusable bags. Then, if you really need another bag, you could buy a paper one for 10 cents.

ADVOCACY CENTRAL

Keep going! You're finishing Step 2 of Advocacy Central!

DISCOVER YOUR INNER CHILD

Exams. Grades. College applications. Job. References. Family commitments. Drama with friends. Feeling too responsible? Too grown up? Too stressed?

You are never too old to reconnect with your inner child. So let her out to play!

When is the last time you:

- Skipped (Yes, skipped. Remember that feeling?)

- Bought bubbles and spent a half-hour sitting and blowing them

- Swooped down a slide

- Rolled down a hill

- Colored in a coloring book or doodle pad (Maybe along to music?)

- Played a board game or cards (Remember Spit and Crazy Eights?)

- Finger-painted

- Made a sand castle

- Played with clay

- Built a course for matchbox cars and let 'em roll

- Played tag. Red light/green light, "Mother May I?"

- Jumped double-dutch

- _____Add your own

- _____Add a friend's

- _____Add your mom's or aunt's

1939 **Josefina Fierro de Bright** organizes protests against racism in the Los Angeles school system, especially against Mexican Americans. She helps Luisa Moreno organize a national Latino congress and becomes its executive secretary. In 1942, when 22 Mexican-American youths are unjustly convicted of murdering a young man, she is crucial in establishing a defense committee. In 1944, the convictions are reversed on appeal.

take 5

Now, pick your favorite inner-child activities and do them! Better still, get with your friends—just the ones you feel absolutely, positively safe with—and have a whole afternoon/ night/weekend/campout to let loose your inner children.

What do you learn/gain by being a little goofy?

....

....

....

....

....

....

How can releasing your inner child—and the feelings you get from doing so—help you?

....

....

....

....

....

....

VOICES FOR GOOD: WOMEN ADVOCATES THROUGH THE YEARS

1939 **Dorothy Schiff** purchases a controlling interest in the New York Post and, in 1942, takes over as publisher. She is the first woman to run a major New York paper. For the next 37 years, after nursing the Post through financial losses that nearly bankrupt her, she turns it into a profitable enterprise dedicated to progressive causes.

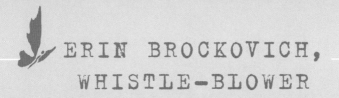

ERIN BROCKOVICH, WHISTLE-BLOWER

In the 1990s, while working as a file clerk at a law firm, Erin Brockovich came across medical records that documented the deteriorating health of many residents of Hinkley, California. Strange, for sure. Coincidence? Maybe not. She brought it to the attention of her boss, Edward Masry, and got his permission to do some more research.

Brockovich couldn't have dreamed up what she discovered next. A toxic, cancer-causing chemical from a local gas and electric company had leaked into the water, and Hinkleyites' health had been severely compromised because of it.

Brockovich, with Masry, filed a lawsuit against the gas and electric company and, in spite of threats, spearheaded a case that awarded $333 million in damages to more than 600 Hinkley residents. It was one of the largest injury settlements in U.S. history.

No amount of money can ever buy back a life, but advocacy like this can lead to a great prize. Today, consumers get the scoop on cleaning up Earth—and earthlings' health—in part thanks to Brockovich, who operates a blog and a foundation and continues to visit environmentally compromised sites. Brockovich's wing fluttering, by the way, went on to earn its weight—in Oscar gold—for Julia Roberts, star of the big-screen hit "Erin Brockovich."

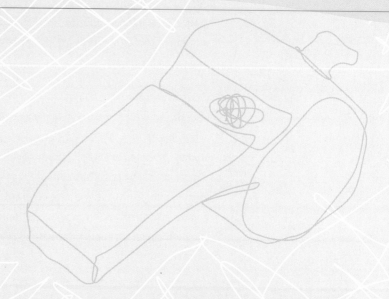

1943 **Eleanor Roosevelt** founds the UN Association of the United States, to work for the creation of the United Nations. Two years later, she is elected chair of the UN Human Rights Commission and helps draft the Universal Declaration of Human Rights. Her advocacy is manifold: She's an ardent opponent of racism, vocal civil rights activist, exemplar of female equality, and policy adviser to several presidents.

Step 3: Harmonize

Now that you've identified an issue, figured out one angle of it, and have a load of research under your belt, you've got a great running start. So concentrate on your "whos." Who could join you and be involved? What do they think about your proposed solutions for your angle of your chosen issue? Do you need to adjust anything? That's what harmonizing is all about.

For example, if your issue is stopping the use of plastic grocery bags at your local supermarket, your partners might be concerned community members, local environmental groups, local natural-food grocers—and maybe even all the area grocers who might like to save some money by not giving away so many bags.

Having support from a number of individuals and organizations is critical to influencing public policy and achieving lasting change. And since you're a high school student, this step of identifying partners is especially important. It'd be great if you could advocate on this forever, but just in case you have other things to tend to (like homework), now's the time to hand off some of the advocacy work to individuals or organizations you've ID'd as your partners.

A is for alliances, which you build along the way. B is for brilliant—the way you'll feel when you combine your brainpower with a network of partners who share your cause. And B is also for brainstorm, which you and your partners will do.

VOICES FOR GOOD: WOMEN ADVOCATES THROUGH THE YEARS

1946

Emily Greene Balch wins the Nobel Peace Prize for her work with the Women's International League for Peace and Freedom, the oldest women's peace organization, having inherited the mantle of the Woman's Peace Party. The league's aim is "to work for permanent peace" and to oppose oppression and exploitation by bringing together "women of different political views and philosophical and religious backgrounds."

Forming partnerships can also provide access to more resources, because your network can now spiral out to create a much larger web of support than you could possibly achieve on your own. You might even grow a network that propels you into the next phase of your life. (College? Career? Everyone you meet on this journey is a potential contact.)

Imagine this journey building you a network offering resources and opportunities for the rest of your life.

SUSANA TRIMARCO DE VERON: WHEN THE PERSONAL BECOMES PUBLIC

It's got to be a mother's worst nightmare: Marita Veron, an artsy 23-year-old with side-swept bangs and a megawatt smile, was kidnapped less than a block away from her home in San Miguel de Tucuman, Argentina, in April 2002. When her mother, Susana Trimarco de Veron, learned that Marita had likely been forced into prostitution by the kidnappers, she began to troll bars and alleys in rough, dangerous neighborhoods, looking for anyone who might know her daughter's whereabouts.

Trimarco de Veron's search and her work with police enabled her to help free 100 young women from bondage, and bring many of the perpetrators to justice—even as she received false leads and death threats. She also formed a network of mothers of missing children and established a shelter for abused women. Trimarco de Veron was able to take her passionate wish for her daughter's return and turn it into a force of advocacy for the people who need it most.

In March 2007, Trimarco de Veron was honored with one of the first International Women of Courage Awards, inaugurated by U.S. Secretary of State Condoleezza Rice. But her wing-flapping isn't done yet: Trimarco de Veron created a foundation that helps human trafficking victims be reintegrated into society; advocates for stronger governmental policies to combat human trafficking; raises awareness in the media; and trains judges, prosecutors, and law officials. Trimarco de Veron will continue to help the Argentine government—and the world—become more involved with the problem of human trafficking. And, of course, she wants to find Marita and bring her home.

WHO'S ON YOUR LIST?

Susana Trimarco de Veron reached out and made alliances with people she never would have met had her life not changed so dramatically: the police, the government, her community, including the victims of abuse. As an advocate, you will meet many new people and make new connections. You will also discover that people you already know feel just as strongly about your issue as you do.

Some suggestions for people you could reach out to include:

- Extended family

- Friends/ casual acquaintances/ friends of friends

- Girl Scout groups and alumnae
- Girl Scout council (staff, girls, volunteers)

- Student-council members

- School principal

- Student body

- Members of organizations you belong to

- School-board members/ superintendent

- Local religious groups

- City agencies/offices

- Local business owners

- Members of organizations already involved in this issue

VOICES FOR GOOD: WOMEN ADVOCATES THROUGH THE YEARS

1949   **Simone de Beauvoir** publishes *The Second Sex*, which is perhaps best summed up by her statement: "One is not born, but rather becomes, a woman." In her view, women have no specific feminine nature but are subject to men's definition of them as "the other"—that is, not male, and therefore regarded by men as an aberration and subordinated as a group with a false aura of "mystery."

Go back to Community Connections and Building a List of Allies, on pages 37 and 50. You already have a full list. Now go to Advocacy Central, and fill in the names of your partners and their contacts. Your family, friends, classmates, coworkers, teachers, coaches, or religious leaders may have even more connections to give you. Use the partners list to keep track of all the people you have met so far on your advocacy journey, and their connections. Think of people you know through friends, family, clubs, school, or organizations who have skills or experience that may be helpful for addressing your issue (such as a family friend who is a videographer, the journalism teacher at your school, or the worker at City Hall who knows your aunt). Remember your Girl Scout alumnae network from page 35 and all of the people you have met in your research. Now, in Advocacy Central, put a P beside the names of those who are potential partners.

CONNECT THE DOTS

Congratulations! Look at all your potential partners! Now, get your partners engaged in your advocacy effort.

Here are a few tips:

- Looking at your list, who are your most important partners for the issue and solution you noted in Advocacy Central? Which partners do you most want to loop into your network (for now or for the future)?

- Based on what you know about their schedules, what kind of first meeting makes sense? Afternoon? Weekend? In-person? Online?

- How can you quickly share your zest for the issue and get your partners to be equally enthusiastic?

 1951   **Bette Nesmith Graham** creates a typewriter correction fluid and markets it herself after IBM refuses to buy it. She makes it with an electric mixer in her kitchen and sells it as Mistake Out before renaming it Liquid Paper. By 1979, when the Gillette Corporation buys her company, she has 200 employees making 25 million bottles of fluid per year. Her will leaves $25 million to a think tank to explore world problems.

61

- Can you start filling in some "To-Dos" on Advocacy Central? Maybe make a copy, mark it "Draft," share it with your partners, and get them to add to it?

- How can you create an opportunity for each partner to make a realistic personal commitment to the cause?

- What do you need to find out/get from your partners, and how can you make the best use of their time?

- Who would be willing to pick up next steps, if there are next steps when your journey ends?

If your mood is "social butterfly," you might "do up" a launch event—almost like a party (but with info and discussion added on). It'll get you and your partners revved up. Or there's always the "virtual launch," where you can rally together online. Any way you do it, the point is this: Trade information with your partners, get a team engaged with you, and get their support identifying, meeting, and "pitching to" the next step—the all-important VIPs!

ADVOCACY CENTRAL   Fill it in!—your partners and some of your to-dos.

AN ADVOCATE WHO NEVER HEARD "NO"

Persuading partners to join her cause was something Juliette "Daisy" Gordon Low, the founder of Girl Scouts, was an expert at. She just didn't take no for an answer, and that sometimes meant she resorted to playing up her deafness. For example, in 1911, when about to leave London to return to America, she needed someone to look after one of the troops of Girl Guides she had started there. She chose Rose Kerr, a woman she barely knew, who turned down the invitation, saying she had no time, wasn't good with girls, and didn't even live in London. "Then that is settled," Daisy said. "The next meeting is on Thursday and I have told them you will take it."

It's been acknowledged that Daisy knew how to zero in on the right partners. Even those who tried to say no often ended up being key figures in Girl Scouting. Anne Hyde Choate, who insisted she had absolutely no time for Girl Scouting, went on to be a vice president and a key builder of the Movement. Another recruit, Ruth McGuire, recalled of Daisy, "She would give such a charming smile as she put away her hearing aid and thanked her victim for her cooperation, assuring her that she was sure she would be most successful and would find the work both interesting and enjoyable."

TRACY REESE, HEART-SMART FASHIONISTA

Designer Tracy Reese's "feminine chic" clothes are often inspired by main events of the past. But there's one vintage accessory that will never appear near any of her runways: cigarettes. Reese has banned all backstage smoking at her shows. And how's this for a model idea? She supplies knitting kits for models to use as an alternative break to smoking while they're getting ready to work the runway. A nonsmoker herself, Tracy partnered with the American Legacy Foundation, an antismoking group dedicated to building a world where young people reject tobacco and anyone can quit. What's more, the Detroit native designed a limited-edition T-shirt to help raise money for the group. "Smoking should not be seen as a sexy accessory, and it is my personal mission to change that conception and build up confidence in young women so they don't cave in to peer pressure," Reese says. She is not only one of a handful of successful black female fashion designers, she's one of the few big names in fashion using her clout on the runway to make a difference in the world. Now that's fluttering some wings.

1955   **Rosa Parks**, a 42-year-old seamstress, triggers the Montgomery Bus Boycott when she refuses a bus driver's order to give up her seat to a white man. The boycott was planned earlier by Martin Luther King Jr. and others, but they needed an inspiring symbol to spark mass protests. The soft-spoken Parks more than fills the bill with her quiet act of courage that brings thousands into the streets and draws the attention of millions worldwide.

take 5

SIX DEGREES OF SEPARATION

You may not be friends with everyone in your school, but you're probably connected to them in a surprisingly close way. Researchers studying human interconnectedness and "social capital" (the advantage a person gains from relationships with others) have developed a theory that everyone in the world is separated, on average, by only six links. As the saying goes, "It's a small world."

Consider this: There are 6 billion people on Earth. If there are six degrees of separation, that's the 6th root of 6,000,000,000—which is 42. Is it reasonable to expect that one person will know 42 people? Yes! Given the Internet and our ability to connect globally through it, it may even be possible to go to the 5th root of 6 billion. That answer, math mavens?*

A popular game that emerged from all this is "Six Degrees of Kevin Bacon." Invented by college students in the early 1990s, the game is simple: Players pick any actor in film history and then link that actor with Kevin Bacon through the films they've been in with Bacon's co-stars until they end up at Kevin Bacon himself. For example, here's a quickie with just two links:

Val Kilmer starred in "Top Gun" with Tom Cruise; Tom Cruise starred in "A Few Good Men" with Kevin Bacon. Therefore, Val Kilmer's "Bacon Number" is 2.

Pick another actor and try doing it yourself with the fewest links and as quickly as possible:

Actor: _____

Bacon Number: _____

In 2007, Kevin Bacon made good on the game that bears his name and launched SixDegrees.org in partnership with Network for Good, AOL, and Entertainment Weekly. The Web site builds on the "small world" phenomenon to create a charitable social network where people can donate to a number of linked charities (some of which are favorite charities of celebrities, such as Hilary Duff and Kanye West). Bacon encourages everyone to be a celebrity for their own favorite causes by joining the Six Degrees movement.

* The 5th root of 6 billion is about 90 (90.2880451). How likely is it that someone knows 90 people? For some people, very likely.

VOICES FOR GOOD: WOMEN ADVOCATES THROUGH THE YEARS

1960 **Jane Goodall** sits alone for months in the jungle habitat of wild chimpanzees, waiting for them to be comfortable with her presence. This enables her to observe them not only using tools but making them— a revolutionary discovery. Goodall becomes the foremost authority on chimpanzees. Today, the Jane Goodall Institute is devoted to nature conservation and environmental education in 96 countries.

Make it yours.

Effective leaders gather input from their team, give credit and praise where and when it's due, and share information—openly and clearly. To be effective, leaders can be quiet, influencing through their actions rather than their voice. Do you know any leaders who take a quiet approach? Effective leaders can be loud, too, but in a good way. Bossy, "my way or the highway" leaders often cause resentment. Why is that?

....

....

Leaders who guard their ideas and take credit (or worse, steal credit) are also doomed. Can you guess why?

....

Think of the people you consider leaders. Who is most effective at reaching her goals?

....

As you network, you're bound to form even more ideas about leadership. In Girl Scouts, the leadership philosophy of Discover, Connect, and Take Action implies that leadership happens from the inside out. It stresses the importance of embracing who you are, connecting with others, and working collaboratively to make things better for all. How does this philosophy apply to this advocacy journey and your efforts with partners? How does it apply to the rest of your life?

....

....

....

....

....

1962 **Dolores Huerta** cofounds (with Cesar Chavez) the National Farm Workers Association, later to become the United Farm Workers (UFW). In 1965, she directs its nationwide grape boycott, which lasts until 1971. It results in a union contract for grape workers and eventually for other migrant farm workers. Huerta also organizes for women's equality, minority voting rights, and progressive judicial nominations.

Step 4: Identify the Big Ears

Your next challenge as an advocate is to identify the VIPs who need to hear about your issue and can take action for change. Who's on the "Who's Who" list when it comes to moving your issue and solution forward? Is it a state issue? Something for the school board? The superintendents or principals in your school district? Members of a special committee of a local governing body? Members of Congress? The board of directors of a local nonprofit organization? The executives of a corporation or chain?

Remember: You're not just looking for bigwigs; you want the right bigwigs—those who can act on your solution. So analyze carefully. If you bring an issue about trees to the parks department only to find out that the city planning commission "owns it," you've misspent your energy—and you're back to the VIP drawing board.

Also keep in mind that those who care about your issue may not be the ones who can influence it. Influencers might be formal (elected or appointed to a role)—or informal, as in someone who has some power because of reputation or celebrity status.

If you've determined that your issue is "owned" by a particular person, you might talk with that person directly. But most likely you'll speak with the official's staff—or the staff of the staff.

Identifying VIPs is a key role for your partners, so get them involved. Their connections and yours add up to a whole lot of potential. You may not have time or be able to get to all the VIPs for your issue. The point is to identify at least one or two to whom you can pitch your solution. Turn the page to see the range of possibilities.

A is for accepting, which you want VIPs to be.
B is for boost, which VIPs will give your cause.

1963

Betty Friedan publishes *The Feminine Mystique*, attacking the belief that homemaking and childbearing are the only ways for women to find satisfaction in their lives. She postulates that a system requiring women to find their identity solely as wives and mothers stunts them. The book, which grew out of a questionnaire Friedan sent her 1942 Smith College graduating class, galvanizes the women's movement.

City council/mayor

Local chamber of commerce/service group (Rotary Club, Lions, Elks)

Local parks and recreation department

Local college/university

Local sororities

Local executive director of nonprofit organization(s)

County government

State representatives/senators

State commissions

Statewide Girl Scout events/organizations

State agency/association/organization

Local, state, and national media (radio, newspaper, TV, Web sites)

Governor

Regional organizations

U.S. representative(s)/senator(s)

National business leaders

National associations/organizations

Girl Scouts of the USA

Federal agencies

U.S. president

Global outreach could include (but isn't limited to):

Ambassadors

United Nations

U.S. military

WAGGGS

Leaders of your community's sister city (if it has established one)

Rotary International

NGOs (nongovernmental organizations)

VOICES FOR GOOD: WOMEN ADVOCATES THROUGH THE YEARS

1966   **Betty Friedan and Pauli Murray**, the first black woman Episcopal priest, write the mission statement for the National Organization for Women (NOW), which they start with 26 other men and women. Its purpose, they declare, is "to take action" so women can gain "full participation in the mainstream of American society now . . . in truly equal partnership with men." Today, NOW's top priorities include an end to violence against women.

WHO'S IN CHARGE OF THE ISSUE?

Review your research and then answer the following questions to identify local and national organizations, politicians, media outlets, and youth groups that could lead to important VIPs.

Who has influence on this issue to move your solution forward?

....

....

....

....

Who are the decision-makers for this issue?

....

....

....

Who do you need to inform or convince before you can move forward?

....

....

....

....

Who else is working or has worked on this issue?

....

....

....

....

FOCUSING IN

Let's pick up on the grocery-bags issue from page 58. You've got some partners:

- Local environmental organizations
- Shoppers who agree with you
- Neighborhood improvement committees
- Local merchants who want to save money by not giving out bags

You gather your partners together and they help you flesh out your plan, so you are now advocating for the supermarket to stop the wasteful use of bags. Specifically, you'll propose that:

- The supermarket will get one of the big food companies to donate reusable cloth bags, which will be handed out during a "giveaway week."

- The local media will be invited to a news conference where the project is announced (which leads to good publicity for the supermarket and the food company donating the bags).

- After the giveaway week, customers still wanting a bag will be charged 10 cents per bag for a paper bag.

Now it's time to find your VIPs, the ones who can really get behind your issue. Who might your VIPs be? Revisit Advocacy Central and put a V next to each potential VIP. Then put a star beside all the VIPs you could realistically approach. Being prepared for how VIPs will respond to you is extremely important. Let's go back to the issue of the grocery bags. On the next page is a flow chart of what might happen, including pushback you might get from VIPs—the questions they might ask and how you might respond. See if you can fill in the empty spaces in the chart to show even more possible pushback and how you would respond.

VIP	POSSIBLE RESPONSES OF VIP	NEXT STEPS	NEXT POSSIBLE RESPONSES OF VIP	FURTHER NEXT STEPS
Manager of local grocery store you want to target	"On board! I'll ask my food-company contacts to pitch in."	SOLVED! Move ahead with your plan.		
	"Sorry, I don't have the authority to set in motion that kind of policy."	ASK: Who else could you refer me to? Get contact info for district or regional manager, or official at corporate HQ, and reach out.		
	"Sorry, you need to talk to my district manager."	Get contact info for district manager and reach out.		
	"But my customers like the plastic bags. They don't cost me much, and they keep my customers happy."	Have environmental pitch ready, and emphasize the handiness of reusable bags. The manager and her store will be viewed as "going green," a benefit to the community—and to the store's reputation!		

As an advocate, you'll often find that policy issues involve VIPs in elected offices. Way back in fourth grade, you learned about state and local governments. How much do you remember? If you need to brush up on U.S. government and civics, that's OK. As you savvy up, pass on what you learn to others. The more people understand the governance process and the importance of public participation, the more they might be able to influence positive change.

1. NAME THE THREE BRANCHES OF THE FEDERAL GOVERNMENT.

2. WHAT MAJOR POLITICAL EVENT TAKES PLACE EVERY FOUR YEARS?

3. WHAT ARE THE NAMES OF YOUR STATE'S TWO U.S. SENATORS?

4. WHO IS YOUR MEMBER OF THE U.S. HOUSE OF REPRESENTATIVES?

5. WHICH POLITICAL PARTY HAS A DONKEY AS ITS SYMBOL?

WHICH PARTY HAS AN ELEPHANT?

6. HOW OLD DO YOU HAVE TO BE TO VOTE?

7. WHO IS THE GOVERNOR OF YOUR STATE?

WHO ARE YOUR STATE AND LOCAL ELECTED OFFICIALS? (REMEMBER, THESE MAY BE THE FIRST PEOPLE YOU SEEK OUT AS YOU ADVOCATE FOR CHANGE!)

8. WHAT IS A KEY ISSUE IN YOUR LOCAL GOVERNMENT RIGHT NOW?

9. IN WHAT CITY IS YOUR STATEHOUSE OR STATE CAPITOL?

10. HOW MANY WOMEN NOW HOLD A STATEWIDE OFFICE IN YOUR STATE? WHAT ARE THEIR NAMES?

WHAT'S YOUR STAGE?

To plan your pitch (see next section), you need to know where you will be delivering it. Will you set up a special meeting with your VIPs or do you need to get on the agenda of their regularly scheduled meeting? If your VIPs are booked, do they have any staff or committee members you could meet with? Maybe one of your partners is involved in an organization that already has a meeting set up. Can you get on the agenda?

Will you have "15 minutes of fame" in the office of an elected official, perhaps with one of the staff members? Will you have a chance to use a PowerPoint presentation or show a short video clip?

Tough questions? That's why you have partners. Get their advice about how to gain access to your VIPs.

1968 **Shirley Chisholm**, representing a New York City district, becomes the first black woman elected to Congress. She hires an all-female staff and speaks out for women's rights. "Women in this country," she says, "must refuse to accept the old, the traditional roles and stereotypes." Three years later, she runs for the Democratic presidential nomination. "I am, was, and always will be a catalyst for change," she says.

Step 5: Plan the Perfect Pitch

So, your partners are organized and you've ID'd your VIPs. Now it's time to put your advocacy message together. You need to define your issue in a compelling way and propose a workable and realistic solution. Refer back to Step 5 of Advocacy Central on page 11.

- Why does your issue matter? Clearly define the issue and focus on the angle your solution addresses.

- Why should VIPs care? Provide a compelling reason: Create the bait, get it on the hook, and reel them in.

- Is your solution reasonable and doable? Offer a realistic solution that translates into action your VIPs can take.

- Show the benefits: for you, me, and the community.

- Make your pitch irresistible. Invite the VIPs to agree with your solution (or offer a better one).

- What questions might come up? How will you answer them? Practice some potential Q&As with your partners.

- Most of all, have faith in your proposed solution and be assertive!

VOICES FOR GOOD: WOMEN ADVOCATES THROUGH THE YEARS

 1971

Katharine Graham, publisher of The Washington Post, rejects a court order to halt publication of the Pentagon Papers, which exposes secrets about the Vietnam War. In 1972, she resists threats by President Nixon to ruin her if she publishes reports, which, as it turns out, lead to his resignation. In her 1998 Pulitzer Prize-winning memoir, *Personal History*, Graham portrays herself as someone who learns to meet the challenges thrust upon her.

Ever listened to a presentation that goes on and on a lot about—well, you're not too sure exactly what? Keep that memory in mind as you plan your pitch. Less is definitely more. Make your pitch pithy.

GOT TALENT? USE IT!

Once you know how you will make your pitch, the fun can really begin. You can showcase your talents and do what comes naturally.

Are you a strong writer or great photographer? Both? Your friend never puts down her video camera? You've got a partner who is a whiz at making PowerPoint presentations or museum-worthy posters? Another who gets the lead in every school play? And another who's a number-cruncher extraordinaire? Put all these talents to use as you build the case for your issue and solution.

Identifying Policy Makers

Here's some advice about how to approach policy makers:

- **Target your efforts.** Survey the policy makers who will be involved in approving the policy or in funding and implementing the program of concern to you. Decide whom to approach and in what order.

- **Do your research.** Know how officials have voted on issues similar to yours. Know their public stance. Know what plans they may have for their futures. Is the VIP you need to approach planning to campaign for a higher public office? Show how a positive stance on your issue would look good to voters—including all the partners you have already amassed.

- **Start with firm supporters** and then move on to those who may be moderately supportive or are undecided on the issue. For example, if you are trying to support a bill pending in the state legislature that would broaden funding for state and local community health services, begin with legislators on the committee that will hear the bill first and members of a friendly caucus, such as the women's caucus. If you are trying to change school-board policy about health curricula, start with the school-board members who might support a more comprehensive approach.

- **Prep for possible questions.** Be prepared for every possible angle of inquiry.

Write It Right

Words can give life and a powerful voice to an issue in a variety of ways:

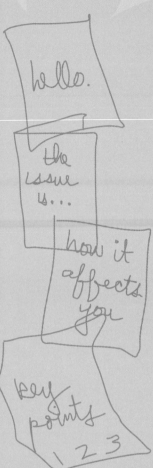

- Draft a letter (on paper or online) to get the meeting, get in the door, or get 15 minutes of time.
- Write a brochure, booklet, or flier to take to a meeting.
- Submit an article to a local newspaper (before or after you make your pitch).
- Create a public service announcement to show at your meeting.
- Write a petition and conduct a signature drive to show how many people care.
- Pull together "talking points" that all your partners can use.
- Write a script or speech for speakers to use in public meetings.

What's Black and White and Read All Over?

Did you know that letters to the editor are the most widely read of anything in a newspaper, after the front page? A letter to the editor is a cost-effective way to raise awareness of your issue. Depending on the publication's readership, your message has the potential to reach hundreds of thousands of people. (Plus, you get to see your name in print!) Give a copy to your VIPs to impress them with how many people you've already reached.

1972 **Billie Jean King** wins the U.S. Open tennis tournament and then speaks out against sexism in sports, vowing not to play in the tournament in 1973 if the women's prize money does not match the men's. Her popularity wields huge influence, and tournament officials agree to equalize the rewards. But her advocacy is most widely felt in federal legislation that ends sex discrimination in high school and college athletics.

When Voice Gets Visual

Artistic additions to your pitch can help make it memorable:

- Design a billboard or flier.

- Perform a skit or play.

- Create a political cartoon.

- Create a short film or documentary.

- Photograph the problem and/or those impacted by it.

- Design a slide show.

Play It Up and Show It Off

If you take photos or make a short video about your issue, consider asking a local gallery or library to feature it. See if you can get your VIPs (or their designees) to attend the showing. Set up a table where you and your partners can recruit more supporters—or ideas to bring to your designated VIPs. Show off the "sign-in" book so everyone can see how many people care.

1976 **Betty Williams and Mairead Corrigan**, cofounders of Women for Peace, get thousands to sign petitions against the violence in Northern Ireland after three children are killed. The two then organize peace marches to mourn the deaths, bringing together tens of thousands of Catholic and Protestant women. Within six months, the violence drops by 70 percent. Their efforts win them the Nobel Peace Prize.

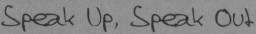

Speak Up, Speak Out

As a speaker, you give voice—literally—to an issue so that others are persuaded to take the action you recommend. Here are some ways to use your voice:

- Meet with elected officials or other policy makers.
- Serve on a task force, committee, advisory board, or youth leadership council.
- Make a phone call.
- Give a speech.
- Hold a news conference.
- Attend a public hearing or city council meeting and ask for the microphone.

you can do it

Speaking Tips

- Elected officials *like* to meet with people they represent, so don't hesitate to set up a meeting (and take partners with you for moral support). You may end up talking to the VIP's staff, but that's still a great way to get your issue and solution on the table.

- Most city council meetings and hearings are open to the public. To speak at a meeting, most city councils and boards only require that you sign up to be on the agenda (which can be as simple as just signing your name). Find out how you can attend a meeting, and then be prepared with your pitch.

VOICES FOR GOOD: WOMEN ADVOCATES THROUGH THE YEARS

1976

Barbara Jordan is the first woman and first black to give the keynote speech at the Democratic National Convention. A congresswoman from Texas, she had already shown her riveting eloquence on national television during President Nixon's 1974 impeachment hearing. The causes she champions throughout her career, such as fair wages and minority voting rights, all benefit from her ability to speak truth to power.

Numbers Game

You can give voice to an issue by documenting it in concrete and factual ways:

- Compile statistics.
- Create a database.
- Conduct an experiment.
- Analyze survey results.
- Design a graph or chart.

Numbers Tips

Use your stats to make your pitch to your VIPs yourself— or "feed" them to your writers, speakers, and visual artists to incorporate into their roles.

Be ready to justify why you chose to analyze and present your data the way you did.

Wangari Maathai creates Kenya's Green Belt Movement, which enables poor women in rural villages to improve their lives by planting trees, an act that combats soil erosion, improves water resources, provides wood fuel for cooking, and earns income from forestry. Maathai expands the movement to include education, health care, and community services. In 2004, she wins the Nobel Peace Prize.

MAP OUT YOUR PITCH

With input from your partners, pick one or two of the ideas given and use them to make an effective pitch. Use the space below to map your pitch and then add it to Advocacy Central.

Write it Right

....

....

....

When Voice Gets Visual

....

....

....

Speak Up, Speak Out

....

....

....

Numbers Game

....

....

....

ADVOCACY CENTRAL   Fill it in! Perfect pitch!

VOICES FOR GOOD: WOMEN ADVOCATES THROUGH THE YEARS

1979   **Mother Teresa**, a Roman Catholic nun from Albania, wins the Nobel Peace Prize for her humanitarian work. Her Missionaries of Charity, founded in 1950 with 13 nuns in Calcutta, India, grows to a global ministry of more than 4,000 nuns who care, in her words, "for the hungry, the naked, the homeless, the crippled, the blind, the lepers—all those people that feel unwanted, unloved, uncared for throughout society."

Make it yours.

Maybe you received an unfair grade or you couldn't get into a class you really wanted. Perhaps it's time to renegotiate some family rules? Or maybe you just really need your friends to understand your point of view. The advocacy steps you are exploring here can apply to your personal life, too. So go ahead, advocate for yourself! Read through the steps below, and then map out your case and keep track of how it went on the next page.

- Zero in on one specific issue; don't try to change everything in one sweep.

- Have some specific solutions or resolutions in mind. Don't just yammer on with every complaint you ever wanted to rip on. And never, ever whine!

- Make your case clear and compelling by doing your research and thinking about lining up the strongest points and facts that support it. For example, for "selling yourself" on a college, job, or scholarship application, you need one strong theme—not an encyclopedia of your life.

- Make your pitch to the right people. For example, if Mom is the one who will decide whether you can drive to school rather than take the bus—because you'll share the car with her—she's the VIP.

- Stay calm, cool, collected, and strong. After all, you're an Ambassador!

 1981 **Sandra Day O'Connor** is the first woman on the U.S. Supreme Court and serves for a quarter century. Her rulings often upset expectations and are the deciding vote time and again. She comes to be seen as the nation's most influential woman on its most controversial issues.

{Advocacy in My Own Life}

→ **YOUR ISSUE** ....

....

→ **YOUR AUDIENCE** ....

....

→ **YOUR CASE** ....

....

→ **PLAN FOR DELIVERING IT** ....

....

→ **HOW DID IT GO?** ....

....

→ **WHAT DID YOU LEARN?** ....

....

→ **WHAT WILL YOU DO DIFFERENTLY NEXT TIME?** ....

....

....

VOICES FOR GOOD: WOMEN ADVOCATES THROUGH THE YEARS

1981 **Martina Navratilova**, the world's top female tennis player, sets a milestone for gay rights with her openness about her sexual orientation. She becomes an activist for gay rights and, in 1992, sues the state of Colorado over a ballot measure denying gays and lesbians protection from discrimination. (The measure is later ruled unconstitutional.)

GET READY TO PITCH

Now, let's get back to your public advocacy pitch. Is it all set?
Got your "talking points" down? All materials and equipment
ready to go? Then follow through:

- If you haven't already, secure a meeting space if
  needed (schools, religious groups, libraries, and youth
  organizations are good possibilities for free meeting
  space).

- Provide a clear agenda and expected outcomes for the
  meeting.

- Share responsibilities. Invite partners to take part in the
  meeting, but be sure everyone is clear on their roles so
  you don't waste the VIPs' precious time.

- Welcome feedback from your partners (remember:
  you chose them for a reason), and honor their diversity
  of strengths, skills, and experience. Hold a dry run and
  make adjustments as needed.

- Show your appreciation to everyone who helps you.
  People will most likely continue their support if they
  know they are appreciated.

- And, yes, think about what to wear! (A is for accessorizing
  correctly, so you fit in at every occasion. B is for borderline,
  something you don't want to be.)

Rigoberta Menchú organizes opposition to Guatemala's repressive government while in hiding in Mexico. Her 1983 oral biography, *I, Rigoberta Menchú*, tells how she grew up in poverty in a Mayan village; how her family was killed by soldiers; and how she took up the struggle for indigenous peasants' rights. The book brings her international recognition and, in 1992, she wins the Nobel Peace Prize.

take 5

ADVOCA-T?

How many logo T-shirts are in your closet? It's easy to see why they're so popular—they're such a clever way to advertise personalities and emotions without saying anything at all! Have you ever designed your own? If not, here's your chance to be a designer and an advocate. Write a slogan or clever saying about your issue on the T. (For example, if you want to pass a "no-kill" law for local animal shelters, you might want to use a cute picture of a puppy with "If you only had 30 days to be adopted, you'd vote 'No kill,' too!"). Get creative with this—maybe even create a REAL Advoca-T-shirt!

1983   **Sally Ride** orbits Earth as the first U.S. woman astronaut in space. After her flight career, she oversees a major policy initiative, the Ride Report, which advocates exploration of the solar system, an outpost on the moon, and a crewed mission to Mars. "My mission these days," she says in 2007, is "to encourage more girls and young women to go into careers in science and math and technology."

Step 6: Raise Your Voice, Make Your Pitch

Leaders speak and then assume that their constituents will:

> Understand
>
> Agree
>
> Care
>
> Act accordingly

The communication gap often caused by these "Four Fatal Assumptions" can be overcome by communicating on three channels—facts, emotions, and symbols—so the message resonates with all listeners.

—From *The Leader's Voice* by Boyd Clarke and Ron Crossland

So now it's time to visit your VIPs and grab their attention. Whether you have a small talk in a conference room or a few minutes at a public meeting, make your pitch to the VIP (or two or many more) who can influence the issue and create a solution. Pitch it using the information and visuals you have prepared.

never assume

THE PERFECT PRESENTATION

- Introduce yourself and why you are there.
- Explain what you hope will happen after the presentation.
- Use talking points in sequential order to present your information.
- Include evidence that supports your point of view.
- Summarize what you want everyone to remember.
- Describe the action you would like them to take.
- Thank them for their time.

Talking Tips

- If you are making the presentation with others, <u>make sure your "roles" are clear.</u> Decide ahead of time who will answer questions.
- <u>Practice</u> ahead of time, and practice some more. Prep for questions, too.
- <u>Don't memorize.</u> Imagine you're having a conversation with good friends who agree with what you are saying.
- <u>Put your talking points on index cards.</u> Even if you have a PowerPoint to follow, equipment can fail, but your index cards can keep you on track.
- But <u>try not to read.</u> Being yourself with a few fumbles is far better than head down, eyes glued to your paper, and reading in a monotone.

more →

A is for attentive, that's how you want your audience.
B is for blown away, which you want those VIPs to be.

More Talking Tips

- Hand out brochures or fact sheets after you speak; otherwise, your audience will be reading, not listening.

- Include at least one story or anecdote that directly relates to your issue. Tell a story that makes people want to help you move forward. Stories give facts a "face."

- Be careful with humor unless you are very practiced and very funny. (And even then, beware. Comedy clubs are full of those who will never be the last comic standing—for very good reasons.)

- Keep your talking points short and sweet. Include only what is relevant and compelling. Nothing makes people tune out faster than lists and lists of numbers, so group your statistics or facts in threes. That will make it easier for people to remember them.

- Create a catch-phrase or memorable line. Borrow a quote—some wording that will stick in your listeners' minds after your presentation is complete.

- Accept that you may be nervous, and use that energy to convey your passion.

- Make eye contact and look at various members of the audience.

- Try not to talk too quickly or too slowly.

- Think "conversational." But try to avoid slang, ums, you knows, and other fillers. (Review page 35, when you recorded your voice.)

- Don't fidget, yawn, or scratch **your nose or other body parts. Try not to slump.**

- Prepare for questions. **Think about what you could be asked and have answers ready. If stumped, say, "That's an excellent question. Let me research that further and get back to you."**

- **If a questioner seems hostile or arrogant,** stay polished, poised, and powerful. **Don't become defensive and don't argue. Try to answer as directly as you can, and then return to important points: what's in it for them, the incredible research you bring to the table. Then ask if anyone else has a question.**

- Be confident. **You've done all your homework.**

- Go for the emotion, **but don't be overly emotional. You don't want to feed into any stereotype of being "a youngster." Fair? Maybe not, but deal with it, and keep your eye on your goal.**

- Research your VIPs **to find any common ground that you share. Does everyone live in the same neighborhood? Does your issue benefit this neighborhood?**

Step 7: Close the Loop

Now that your pitch is done, it's time to tidy things up. You don't want to leave anyone hanging, even if your journey on the road to advocacy ends soon. Passing your effort forward ensures that the good you started will continue.

Ideally, your VIPs commit to a next step, which might be as small as agreeing to read your information in more detail. Or they might assign a staff member to investigate, or suggest another way to address your issue. If all your expectations weren't met, don't be discouraged. Change is hard, and some people are resistant to it. Simply by speaking up, you've made your point and started the fluttering of those butterfly wings. You can return with more partners and more information and even seek out other VIPs who may be more open to your message. Perhaps a portion of your issue will be addressed and that will be enough to spark later, greater change. Be proud of what you've done and how responsible you are in moving your issue forward through others.

ASSESS YOUR PITCH

With your partners, discuss how the meeting went. How effective was the pitch? What went over well? What could have been improved? Who can now carry the effort forward?

....

....

....

....

FOLLOWING UP WITH VIPs

No matter what happened, send out thank-you notes to the VIPs promptly. These give you another chance to make your point (but briefly—these are thank yous, not pitches) and make you memorable. If your pitch went well, use your thank you to detail your expectations and understanding of what the VIPs are doing to promote your cause and how else you can be involved. Consider using snail mail; a handwritten note will make the biggest impact.

take 5

REWARD YOURSELF

Even the powerful and influential know the importance of taking a break. OK, so you don't have a private jet to whisk you off to a secluded tropical island. Reward yourself with a long bike ride, a walk with a friend, an afternoon catching up on the novel you set aside, a manicure and pedicure, a date with friends at your favorite coffee shop, a morning at a museum—whatever relaxes and renews you.

1986

Oprah Winfrey goes national with her Chicago-based talk show. It becomes the most popular talk show ever, and she uses it as a platform for her views and a launching pad for her media empire. Now a multibillionaire, Winfrey has given a reported $303 million to such causes as education, women's empowerment, orphans, literacy, and health care. Her charity organization, Oprah's Angel Network, has raised another $51 million.

Thinking Points

What did it (feel) like to make your pitch to the VIPs?

Did you feel (assertive) and in command of the subject?

Was there (support) for your issue and proposed solution?

Why or why not? How much had to do with your pitch and how much with factors you can't control?

What do you need to do next to make change happen?

What was the most (surprising) or interesting thing you learned?

What was the most (useful) thing you learned?

Now, think about how the pitch—and your whole advocacy journey—went from your own perspective.

Did you develop or use a new skill or talent? If so, what was it?

What action did you take that had the most impact or success? Why do you think it was so successful?

What was the least successful action you took? Why do you think it didn't work?

If you could do one thing on this journey over again, what would it be—and why?

Describe the person you met on this journey who had the biggest impact on your advocacy efforts.

Did you get anything started through your efforts (even the smallest ripple) that you or one of your partners want to continue? What? Why?

What are you "passing on"?

Step 8: Reflect, Reward, Celebrate

> " How wonderful it is that nobody need wait a single moment before starting to improve the world. "
>
> —Anne Frank

> " To me success means effectiveness in the world, that I am able to carry my ideas and values into the world—that I am able to change it in positive ways. "
>
> —Maxine Hong Kingston

VOICES FOR GOOD: WOMEN ADVOCATES THROUGH THE YEARS

1989

Aung San Suu Kyi delivers a speech for democratic freedom as Burmese soldiers, with guns drawn, await orders to fire. She is put under house arrest but continues to oppose the military dictatorship. In 1991, she receives the Nobel Peace Prize "for her nonviolent struggle for democracy and human rights." She gives her $1.3 million prize money to an education fund for the people of Burma (now called Myanmar).

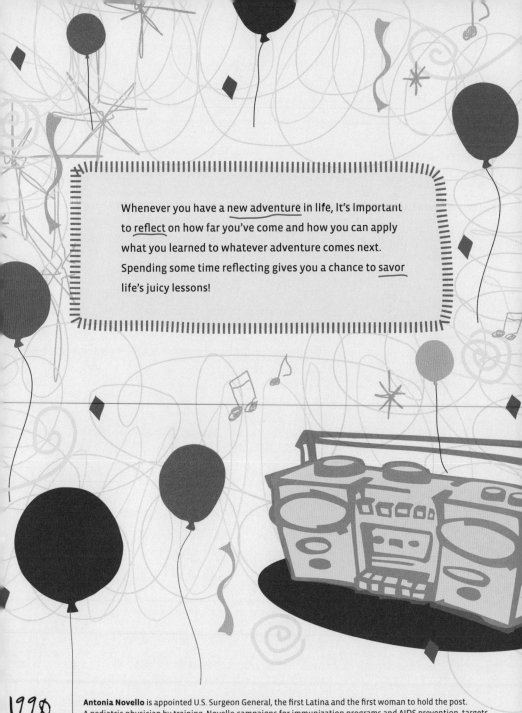

Whenever you have a new adventure in life, It's Important to <u>reflect</u> on how far you've come and how you can apply what you learned to whatever adventure comes next. Spending some time reflecting gives you a chance to <u>savor</u> life's juicy lessons!

Antonia Novello is appointed U.S. Surgeon General, the first Latina and the first woman to hold the post. A pediatric physician by training, Novello campaigns for immunization programs and AIDS prevention, targets underage drinking and smoking, and is especially critical of the tobacco industry for advertising intended to attract youngsters. Joe Camel is her least favorite cartoon character.

Savor the Moments

Along the journey, there were probably less serious moments that may not be represented in the Thinking Points reflection you just did. Random things such as "strangest experience" and "best outfit" deserve mentioning, too, right? So what was the:

- Biggest "duh" moment?
- Strangest experience?
- Best outfit?
- Yummiest snack?
- Most embarrassing moment?
- Worst technological glitch?
- Greatest "aha" moment?
- Greatest giggle moment?

PASS IT ON

Part of closing the loop is letting others know about your effort and its progress—and offering a call to action to those who might step in and carry it forward. A nice way to accomplish this is to combine it with a celebration. Try one of these options:

Option 1: Host an Advocacy Appreciation Event

Organize a meeting at your Girl Scout council, school, or community forum and give your partners a chance to take a next step (or two) in carrying your issue forward. You might also give them something special: a scrapbook, a handmade gift that relates to the issue, a plaque, T-shirt, certificate, or some other token of appreciation. Consider commemorating the occasion with a Girl Scout ceremony.

Option 2: Prepare and Share a Presentation

Prepare a presentation of what you've accomplished, and share it with your VIPs, friends, classmates, family, or community organization. Invite the media to attend or write up a description for the local paper. Include a description of:

- Your issue
- Your research
- Your solution
- The people you helped/what was changed
- Everyone who helped you and what they did

VOICES FOR GOOD: WOMEN ADVOCATES THROUGH THE YEARS

Hillary Clinton heads a task force to reform health care. Her plan mandates that employers provide health coverage to all employees through private health maintenance organizations. Congress rejects the plan. In 2007, as a U.S. Senator from New York, the former First Lady proposes universal health care during her presidential campaign.

Option 3: Get Funky with It

Prepare the same information as Option 2, but do it up in an artistic way. Perform a dance, song, or short play. Or read a poem, or present photographs, paintings, or other art that captures all the elements of your issue and solution.

THANK YOUR LUCKY STARS

Don't forget to thank those who have helped you all along the way by sending thank-you letters or notes in a timely fashion; it's not only polite, but you're much more likely to be remembered in a positive way. And who knows? You may need their help again in the near future if you decide to pursue your advocacy work or if you need a reference for college, scholarship, or job applications.

HIGH FIVE!

One of the greatest things about being a Girl Scout Ambassador is having the chance to communicate the positively powerful Girl Scout message to others in your community. And you just did that—by being an advocate. So CONGRATULATIONS! If you haven't already, why not plan a Girl Scout ceremony to commemorate how far you've come since you first sat down and wrote in this book? Then, spend some time in the next section, reflecting on what you've accomplished, what you've learned, and how you'll use this knowledge in the very near future. Yes, Ms. Ambassador and advocate *extraordinaire*—you've earned it!

ADVENTURES IN ADVOCACY

Have you been bitten by the advocacy bug? Do you want changing the world to be your life's work? Check out some of the careers that can have advocacy as a key element:

Ambassador

Congressperson

Artist

Event organizer

Doctor
(as for Doctors
Without Borders)

Filmmaker

Journalist

Healthcare worker

Fund-raiser/grant writer

Labor-union organizer

Lawyer
(such as for
the American Civil
Liberties Union)

Lobbyist

Mediator

Professor

Public
relations
agent

Member of
local government

Public affairs
officer

Nonprofit
spokesperson
(as for
Girl Scouts!)

Religious leader

Researcher

Senator

Scientist

Social worker

Web master, blogger,
chatroom monitor
—anyone who advances
advocacy efforts via
the Internet

1995

Bette Midler forms the New York Restoration Project, "dedicated," in her words, "to reclaiming and maintaining parks, community gardens, vacant lots—every potential 'green' space that is in disarray." The pop singer helps purchase 114 neglected plots being auctioned by the city. She buys 51 of the most neglected. With gardeners from the New York Garden Trust, she turns them into "urban oases."

Make it yours.

Are there any careers listed that you never even thought about before?

....

....

....

....

Are there any careers listed that you know are definitely not for you? Why not?

....

....

....

....

Choose a career from the list that you know the least about and, with friends, plan a Career Day for which each friend will research one career and then share the information. What do you think of this career as a possibility for you now?

....

....

....

....

2000 **Shirin Ebadi** is arrested in Iran for "disturbing public opinion" and banned from practicing law. She turns her focus from dissidents to the rights of women and children and, in 2002, draws up a law against child abuse. It is approved by the Iranian parliament. In 2003, she wins the Nobel Peace Prize. In 2007, with the ban on her law practice ended, she vows to defend an imprisoned Iranian-American scholar.

Maria Hinojosa's passion for speaking up for those who can't is a natural fit in her career as a journalist. Hinojosa traveled from Africa to India to South America to create the documentary "Child Brides, Stolen Lives" for public television's newsmagazine program, "NOW." The documentary tells the story of women's powerlessness around the world. Learn more about it at www.pbs.org/now/shows/341/facts.html.

As a college student, **Wendy Kopp** saw how to put a dent in educational inequality: recruit outstanding recent college graduates to teach for two years in America's neediest schools. After graduation, Kopp founded Teach for America, a national teacher's corps that now has 5,000 members who reach 440,000 students in low-income communities. Kopp was named one of "America's Best Leaders" by U.S. News & World Report and the Center for Public Leadership at Harvard's Kennedy School of Government.

VOICES FOR GOOD: WOMEN ADVOCATES THROUGH THE YEARS

2002 **Sharon Hom** takes the reins of Human Rights in China, founded by scholars and activists in 1989 just before the lethal crackdown on dissidents in Beijing's Tiananmen Square. A former law professor, Hom quickly focuses on the ethics of companies doing business in China—most recently including Google and Yahoo!, which have been accused of helping the Chinese government censor free speech.

I took the first step and we are all marching on now to great achievements.
—Juliette Gordon Low

What you leave behind is not what is engraved in stone monuments, but what is woven into the lives of others.
—Pericles, ancient Greek politician, general, and statesman

We delight in the beauty of the butterfly, but rarely admit the changes it has gone through to achieve that beauty.   —Maya Angelou

Do you have a favorite quote that has inspired your journey? Write it (or one of your own!) here:

2004
Alice Waters reinvents the meaning of school lunch. Known for her revolutionary Berkeley, California, restaurant Chez Panisse, which uses only local ingredients, she proposes an "edible education" for every Berkeley public school. Students would "plant seeds, raise crops, cook food, and learn about sustainable ecosystems." When the program is fully funded, each school is expected to have its own garden and cafeteria.

THE ABC'S OF AMBASSADOR-ING AND ADVOCACY

A is for **advocate**, which you've become.

B is for **butterfly**, fluttering wings of change.

C is for **courage, confidence**, and **character**—as in the Girl Scout mission, as in you.

B is for Bravo!
You've reached this journey's end!

B is for **bold**, which advocates are. **B** is for **between friends**—share all your moods. **B** is also for **boss**, the best kind, one who brings people together. **B** is for **bottleneck**. Did your issue get caught in one for just a little bit? **B** is for **better**—that's how advocates make the world. And **B** is for **by the way**... this was *some* journey, wasn't it?

Girl Scouting builds girls of courage, confidence, and character, who make the world a better place.

As an Ambassador and advocate, you've got those qualities in abundance. So C is also for

congratulations!

oy a big round of applause.
Maybe even take a bow.

Then, go forth!
Change the world
a little more.

thoughts